God's Consoling Love

G000079013

God's Consoling Love

Sermons and Addresses

MICHAEL MAYNE

Edited, with an introduction by
Joel W. Huffstetler

DARTON · LONGMAN + TODD

This edition first published in 2013 by
Darton, Longman and Todd Ltd
1 Spencer Court
140 – 142 Wandsworth High Street
London SW18 4JJ

**All royalties from sales of this work go to LA FOLIA,
towards their ground breaking opera projects with
special needs children in which everyone's song
is heard and transformed into life-changing
experiences through unique devised performances
www.lafoliamusic.org.**

ISBN 978-0-232-53017-9

A catalogue record for this book is available from the British
Library.

Phototypeset by Kerrypress Ltd, Luton, Bedfordshire
Printed and bound in Great Britain by Bell & Bain, Glasgow.

Contents

Foreword by the Revd Richard Coles ix
Acknowledgements xiii
Introduction by Joel W. Huffstetler xv

1   Holy Week and Easter 1
    Great St Mary's Newsletter, April 1980
    Cambridge

2   A Loving Response to God 3
    Christian Stewardship Conference,
    14 July 1982
    King Alfred's College, Winchester

3   Easter People 9
    Easter Day, 1983
    Great St Mary's, Cambridge

4   Bread for the Starving and Water to the
    Parched 16
    Third Sunday of Easter, 1983
    Great St Mary's, Cambridge

5   Mr Botha's Visit 20
    Great St Mary's Newsletter, June 1984
    Cambridge

6   The Eighteenth Camel 23
    12 January 1986
    Great St Mary's, Cambridge

7   **The Kingdom of God**   27
    Preached before the civic dignitaries
     of the Greater London Area,
    7 September 1986
    Westminster Abbey

8   **Unconditional, Fathomless, and
    Ours for the Asking**   34
    Address for a Day of Prayer, 4 February 1989
    Westminster Abbey

9   **God's Consoling Love**   39
    5 February 1989
    Westminster Abbey

10 **Uncalculating, Indiscriminate,
    Unconditional Love**   42
    25 February 1990
    Westminster Abbey

11 **Whatever You Do, I Love You**   46
    30 June 1991
    Westminster Abbey

12 **Anger**   51
    11 February 1996
    Pembroke College Chapel, Cambridge

13 **Remember**   58
    16 February 1997
    Southwark Cathedral

14 **Word Become World**   65
    Annual Shakespeare Sermon, 26 April 1998
    Holy Trinity Parish, Stratford

15   **The Greatest Drama of All**   78
      Actors' Church Union Centenary, 25 April 1999
      Cotham Parish, Bristol

16   **A Ministry of Love**   85
      Ordination of Deacons Service, 4 July 1999
      Birmingham Cathedral

Foreword

The late eighties, early nineties, were the best of times, the worst of times. For me they began in a band which, rather ambitiously, sought to bring down Margaret Thatcher with pop music while advancing the cause of gay liberation. Although more successful in the latter than the former, we nevertheless sold a great many records on the way. This triumph coincided with a catastrophe, the arrival of HIV which devastated our generation in the decade that followed. Early in the nineties I lost a dear friend, Hugo Irwin, and wrote about his death in a newspaper, a death that was not without grace, a grace that caught me by surprise.

I was never able, quite, to shake off that surprising grace and, after some twists and turns, ten years later I was ordained in the Church of England. A week or two before the great day an envelope arrived with a Salisbury postmark and when I opened it the letterhead revealed it was from the Dean Emeritus of Westminster, The Very Reverend Michael Mayne, KCVO. I couldn't imagine why so exalted a churchman was writing to so lowly an ordinand, but I read on and discovered that he had heard of my forthcoming ontological alteration from a common friend and wanted to wish me happiness and fulfilment in my ministry – and to thank me for the piece I had written ten years earlier.

Michael back then, very much involved with the pastoral care of those with HIV/AIDS, had quoted from my article in a Three Hour Address for Good Friday at Westminster Abbey and in a chapter for his book, *Learning to Dance*. I had no idea the words I'd written were spoken among the tombs of kings and reprinted in the writings of so eminent a churchman and respected a preacher. I wish I had, because I might have got to know him, and to thank him for the generosity and compassion he had shown to a community beyond the margins of sympathy of many at the time, all the more remarkable for coming from a figure at the heart of the Establishment. Generosity and compassion always informed Michael's ministry, his preaching and his writing, and you will find much evidence of them within these pages. His was a ministry of love – the word alone appears 168 times in the text, I checked – love poured out abundantly, in a movement and spirit that is faithful to the example of Jesus Christ, the pattern of priests and deacons and deans and bishops. In these sermons we encounter love in the fight against apartheid, among the colleges of Cambridge and the cloisters of Westminster Abbey, in a walk by a river, in a childhood long gone, in the teaching of a peculiar anchoress on the outskirts of Norwich in the fourteenth century, in inner city London in the early sixties, and finally - fittingly - in an address to those about to be ordained deacon, as I was back in 2005 when his letter arrived.

Michael died only a year later and I did not get to know him and Alison personally; but I have since discovered that there was more overlap in our lives than I had thought. We had both been involved in the Lighthouse, the first dedicated facility in London for people with HIV/AIDS; we both worked at the BBC, Michael as head of Religious Programming for radio, me as a jobbing presenter; we were both born in Northamptonshire, he the son of a parson, me the son of a shoemaker. And there was one more overlap; some time after I came to be Priest in Charge of Finedon I fell into conversation with a parishioner who told me that a clergyman and his family had a holiday home here years ago. He couldn't remember who he was, but he definitely had something to do with Westminster Abbey and he thought he might have been called Michael. Of all the parishes, in all the dioceses, in all the world ....

I am sorry I missed him in Finedon, I am sorry I missed him in life, but I am grateful to encounter him so powerfully in these sermons, and to explore with him 'the secret of the universe revealed in the alphabet of human words and actions, the words and actions of (Jesus Christ), who revealed, both in his life and his death, the breath-taking power of God's mercy and the meaning of unlimited forgiveness'.

The Revd Richard Coles
Parish Priest, St Mary the Virgin, Finedon

Acknowledgements

The sermons and addresses contained in this volume were first read and evaluated during a sabbatical in 2009. I am ever thankful to the people of St Luke's Episcopal Church, Cleveland, Tennessee for their gracious offer of sabbatical time. Serving as rector of St Luke's remains a great privilege and joy.

My thanks to Andrea Spraggins, Parish Administrator of St Luke's, for her help in the production of this volume.

David Moloney, Editorial Director of Darton, Longman and Todd, has been supportive of this project at every turn and has my gratitude for his commitment to bringing more of Michael Mayne's work into print.

My wife, Debbie, has been supportive of, and involved in, the production of this volume at every stage, including the re-typing of each of these pieces for submission to DLT, maintaining the spelling and punctuation from Michael Mayne's original manuscripts. Thank you, my love.

Alison Mayne has been supportive of my work on her husband's papers ever since I first contacted her in 2008. Thank you, Alison, for your every kindness, and for making possible more of your husband's work reaching grateful readers. This book is dedicated to you, to Mark, and to Sarah.

JWH

Introduction

In 2010 *To Trust and to Love: Sermons and Addresses*, the first volume of Michael Mayne's previously unpublished sermons and addresses, received a warm reception by readers not only in Great Britain, but around the world. During his lifetime, Mayne published five major books. Since his death in 2006, two more volumes have been added to his body of work, *To Trust and to Love* and also *Prayer*, a collection of addresses Mayne offered during Westminster Abbey's annual Day of Prayer in 1996. *God's Consoling Love: Sermons and Addresses*, now marks the third addition to the growing body of published material by one of the finest priests of his generation.

Michael Clement Otway Mayne (born 1929) was ordained in 1957, and served the church in a variety of capacities until his death in 2006. During his career, Mayne served as a parish priest, diocesan staff member, and broadcasting executive. In 1986, Mayne began his ten-year tenure as Dean of Westminster. Mayne's retirement years were filled with guest preaching invitations, as well as speaking engagements at conferences and retreats, including regular trips to the United States. He was a much sought after spiritual director during the retirement years and published three books during this period, including *The Enduring Melody*, released just a month before his death from cancer of the jaw.

During his lifetime Michael Mayne did not seek to publish a volume of his sermons. In his book *Pray, Love, Remember*, in preparing to quote from a sermon he had given in Westminster, Mayne observes, 'Sermons do not travel well. They are spoken in a particular context to a particular congregation, and the freshest of words too quickly become stale.' Oftentimes true; yet some sermons do stand the test of time, and their messages endure and can offer insight, encouragement and hope long after that first 'particular congregation' has dispersed.

After a guest preaching appearance of Mayne's in Boston, Massachusetts, a grateful member of the 'particular congregation' that day, who had traveled from Ontario, Canada to hear Mayne, wrote to him a letter of appreciation for the sermon. Her comments included, 'Such fine preaching deserves to be heard by many.' This second volume of previously unpublished sermons and addresses is offered in the firm belief that she was right.

Joel W. Huffstetler
25 June 2013
Cleveland, Tennessee

1

Holy Week and Easter

GREAT ST MARY'S NEWSLETTER,
APRIL 1980

Cambridge

Every year I am more certain. You can learn more about God and his love for you, understand more about the ultimate human questions, and be changed more profoundly during the solemn, disturbing and (ultimately) joyful seven days of Holy Week than in the whole of the rest of the year put together.

All the final events of Jesus' life are crowded into these few days. Each day the mood changes – from the crowd's welcome on Palm Sunday, through the companionship of the last shared meal in the Upper Room, to the desolation of Good Friday and the joy of Easter Day. To worship God on Palm Sunday and not again until Easter Day is as unsatisfactory as reading the first chapter and the last page of a great novel, or agreeing to play in a symphony and only joining in the opening bars and the finale. It is to celebrate too easy a victory.

Once *understand* Holy Week and you can never again believe God to be uncompassionate, or be baffled by suffering and evil, or terrified of death.

But I do mean 'understand'. And that means appropriating these events to yourself. Seeing them not just as events in history, but timeless truths – as true for us as for the first disciples, and as capable of changing our lives as they did theirs. We receive our Palm cross for the journey to Jerusalem on Palm Sunday. We take our place at table for the Last Supper on Maundy Thursday. We wait at the foot of the cross and witness the Passion on Good Friday. We renew our baptismal promises on Easter Eve. We find the tomb is empty and Christ risen on Easter Day.

This is not play-acting. This is a slow-motion spelling out and meditating upon those great acts of God we rehearse at each Eucharist. This is how I meet God and respond to his love. This is how I discover what God has to say about *my* life, *my* suffering, *my* death, *my* resurrection.

Please may we celebrate Holy Week *together* this year, especially on Maundy Thursday, Good Friday, Easter Eve and Easter Day?

What I ask is *costly*. Shouldn't it be?

A Loving Response to God

CHRISTIAN STEWARDSHIP CONFERENCE, 14 JULY 1982

King Alfred's College, Winchester

I have in my possession a sermon by an American bishop who shall be nameless and this is his text: 'If we have died with Christ to selfishness, we have risen with him to stewardship.'

He appears to be suffering from a kind of dottiness brought about by too much thinking about stewardship which every stewardship adviser must surely fear. For if we aren't careful, stewardship becomes a kind of all-purpose word, a Humpty Dumpty word which means whatever we choose it to mean, until it comes to mean both everything and nothing. For stewardship is not the Gospel.

Mother Julian of Norwich, that extraordinary fourteenth-century mystic who speaks to so many, sums up the ground of our belief.

Wouldest thou learn the Lord's meaning?
Learn it well:

Love was his meaning.
Who showed it thee? Love.
What showed he thee? Love.
Wherefore showed it he? For love.

This is the truth about God, simple yet almost
overwhelming, which you come to see when your eyes
have been opened. Once you have grasped it, really
heard it and understood it and made it part of yourself,
then it changes everything else. It is spelled out in
the New Testament in one particular human life, in
terms of a man speaking of a Samaritan, a lost sheep,
a rebellious son; in terms of hands laid on a blind
man's eyes or a madman's head; in terms of a towel,
a basin, and a washing of feet; a loaf of bread and a
cup of wine; of a wooden cross and an empty tomb
and of a continuing, transforming presence. Being a
Christian means trusting that those words and those
actions are the definitive Word of God; trusting that
the experience of being met and loved and forgiven
is a valid experience of God; for the Christian life is
nothing less than my response to Love.

Yet that response has to be worked out (in William
Blake's phrase) 'In minute particulars'. And it is
in responding to Love in a realistic and therefore
inevitably costly way, that I understand Christian
stewardship. For stewardship is not the Gospel – the
Gospel is what *God* does. Stewardship is that re-
ordering of priorities that follows when you realise
that you are loved; that all you are is the gift of God;

and that by pledging a part of your time and gifts and money you are proclaiming an unpopular minority view of how things truly are.

But what can I tell you of stewardship that you don't already know full well? Nothing, perhaps; yet I want to share what for me is a rich source of insight into the meaning of stewardship, for I find that nowhere are its truths more perfectly and consistently proclaimed than in the Eucharist. Let me explain.

Stewardship is about how we regard matter: 'God likes matter,' wrote C. S. Lewis, 'he invented it.' So, in the first chapters of Genesis, God looks on all he creates and sees it is good; it is his gift to man and it exists so that man may have communion with God. And God blesses everything he creates. That means that everything in creation can become the sign of his presence if only we have eyes to see. Man's place in the world is therefore not that of *owner* but *steward*, given the world on trust with a double duty: thankfully to receive it as a gift and thankfully to offer it back to God; to work upon it, explore it, develop it, live off it, but always to reverence it.

The Greek word for that thanksgiving is Eucharist. And if man is faithful to God's intention then his life will become Eucharist with God for he will live thankfully or eucharistically. But it didn't work. For from the beginning men chose to use the world for their own ends, increasingly relegating God to a small bit of his world – the Temple bit, the sacred bit, the church bit – and claiming the rest as their own.

But God is not so easily diverted. And so there is a new creation. The Word becomes flesh so that God may complete what he has begun. So Jesus uses the natural world to show how everything can be seen as a sign of God's presence; and what is so striking is that at every point – even finally on the cross – Jesus receives his life thankfully from God and offers his life thankfully back to God. So he restores to us the vision of man as the steward or, if you like, the priest of God's creation. And in order to drive the truth home he gives us the Eucharist, through which week by week and day by day Christians act out what they believe in the whole context of thanksgiving. Every time we take the bread and wine, our food and drink 'which earth has given and human hands have made' and give thanks for them, we are setting them in their true relation to God. We are as it were dipping into the world and lifting out of it these symbols of God's natural gifts as worked upon by man. This is what all matter was meant to be, the direct means of contact between God and us, and we are celebrating life itself, saying that it is both our duty and our joy as its stewards to give thanks for it at all times and in all places, whether it is sweet or sour; and so making life a loving response to God.

But stewardship is also about the costly offering of yourself and what is yours. On that last night, at that last supper, Jesus took bread and did four things with it: he took it in his hands, he thanked God for it, he broke it, he shared it. And he said: 'This is me. This is my body. Here is the acted parable of my life: taken and offered back to the Father, lived thankfully, given in costly love and broken on the cross, and shared.' That is the pattern of self-effacing, sacrificial, self-giving love which is the heart of the character of Jesus Christ and therefore of God himself; and the pattern of those who accept his authority and seek to grow in his likeness.

So every Eucharist is a kind of acted parable through which, as we do these actions with bread and wine; taking, giving thanks, breaking, sharing, we are choosing to identify ourselves with the way of self-giving love. Perhaps you know the lovely words of St Augustine:

> You are the Body of Christ ... in you, and through you, the work of the Incarnation must go forward. You are to be taken, consecrated, broken and distributed, so that you may now be ... vehicles of the eternal love.

If then stewardship is at once the recognition that the world is God's, the offering back to God of that which is his already, and our response to the divine love, then stewardship begins and ends here at the Eucharist.

'*My life for you*.' Isn't that in the end what it's about, the birth, the life, the death on a cross? God saying, '*My life for you*'. As we kneel at the communion rail and hear the words 'The body of Christ keep you in eternal life' and know God's life in our own, he is saying: 'My life for you'. Isn't this what he longs for us to say in return: *'My life for you'*, as we assert that life is not a taking but a giving, not an owning but a sharing, not a holding back in fear but a giving of yourself in trust?

It isn't easy to preach the Gospel when you are still so little converted yourself; nor is it easy to be paid to spend your time advising on stewardship when you are still so poor a steward, knowing how little you still give and how much you still keep to yourself. That is why we need constantly to come back to this place of Eucharist where, if we are penitent, we are forgiven, and where we are renewed in this pattern of thanking and giving and sharing which we know in our bones is how things are meant to be. God draws me on, infinitely slowly, waiting for me to respond. For love is his meaning and in the end I shall find him irresistible.

3

Easter People

EASTER DAY, 1983

Great St Mary's, Cambridge

I used to live near a river on the far side of which was an old disused railway track. Very often I would take my dog and walk along the mile of that track till I knew it like the back of my hand. It's good to get to know one's walk really well. You see the river, the fields, the hedgerows in all their varying moods. You notice the shape of trees and the flight of birds. You know that bit of the river where the kingfisher is most likely to be glimpsed; you know the trees where in the winter the long-tailed tits can be seen; you know the bit of track where the wild strawberries grow in June. You observe both the pain and the beauty in nature: the bloodied corpse of a rabbit or a mole, the kestrel diving on a field mouse, as well as the branches of trees at dusk on a winter's evening and the calling of coots, or the profusion of wild roses and scabius and poppies in summer when the fields are thick with corn. But above all you become aware of the constantly changing light, and how at different times and on different days the colour changes in a subtle way. Always one colour predominates: brown or green or cobalt or that kind of bruised purply grey.

You also become aware of the constantly moving life: even in the snow and mud and the apparent deadness of winter the force of new life is working underground, and then through the spring there is the vigour of new growth coming to a glorious summer maturity and then an autumnal decay. Town dwellers that we are, we are still very close to this natural cycle, and there's often a kind of matching pattern in our own lives: not only in the obvious progress from the spring of childhood to the winter of old age, but also in the periods of deadness and pain and the times of new vigour and contentment most of us experience. And it's no accident that the Church's year is based on a similar pattern: a birth at the dead of winter, the long bleak days of Lent, the new life bursting from the tomb at Easter, the outflowing of the Spirit as summer comes, the long, green lazy weeks of Trinity.

So, although we may regret the absence of good Easter cards showing the risen Christ, is it not very natural that they should show spring flowers and lambs and chickens and eggs – and even rabbits? But this identifying of Easter with chickens breaking out of eggs and primroses breaking out of the dark earth is but a very tiny part of the truth of Easter. For we're not here to celebrate spring: we are here to celebrate the risen Christ.

Let me go back for a moment to my analogy of the old railway track. Behind all I've described, the shapes and colours and the changing light, the life and growth of trees and crops and animals, there is one source: one source of every scrap of energy and light and colour which brings the world alive to me and makes it beautiful. And that is the sun. The sun is literally life-giving. Even on the darkest and coldest winter day the sun isn't just another element in the whole scene. It's the power-house making life possible for me and everything around me, and it's also the means of my seeing everything as it truly is.

When the author of the Book of Revelation needed a strong image for the risen Christ he seized on that of the sun. His face, he wrote, 'is like the sun shining in full strength'. And many poets and hymn-writers have likened Christ to the sun.

> Christ, whose glory fills the skies.
> Christ, the true, the only light.
> Sun of righteousness arise.
> Triumph o'er the shades of night.

So wrote Charles Wesley. And John Keble:

> Sun of my soul, thou Saviour dear,
> it is not night if thou be near.

11

St John tells us that it was in the very early morning, just before sunrise, that Mary comes to the garden to bring spices to the tomb. And it is Sunday when he rises: the day of the sun. And you can see why the sun is such a powerful image for the risen Christ. For Good Friday and Easter Day are not just two events in the life of Jesus of Nazareth. They're happenings which, then and now, point to truths about the nature of God which, if you will allow them to, can transfigure the whole world in your eyes. C. S. Lewis said: 'I believe in the resurrection of Christ as I believe that the sun has risen, not because I can look on it direct, but because by it I see everything else.' For those few men and women who knew Jesus in the flesh the experience of knowing that Christ was in their midst, with them forever as a life-giving Spirit, quite simply illuminated and altered all that had gone before: his words, his actions, his cross – all were changed and newly understood in the light of Easter. Like the sun, the risen Christ now becomes the means of their seeing everything as it truly is. It's like being born again, they said: everything has become new. Whereas we were blind, now we see. Whereas we were deaf, now we hear. Whereas we were dead, now we are truly alive. Yet not I, but Christ lives in us.

You can see why it's necessary to keep Christmas and Good Friday and Easter and Whitsun as separate days and relive them every year. For the more you walk the same path the more you notice, so that each year of Easter Day we should be able to say: I never saw this or that truth quite so clearly before. But do we for a moment suppose that the truths expressed in those events are not equally true on every single day of the year? Of course they are. On days of bleakness and depression or during a time of illness or bereavement the sun may be hidden but it is still there, a life-giving force. Christ is still risen, the Lord of life. You may remember those words written by a Jewish prisoner on a wall in a prison in Cologne: 'I believe in the sun even when it is not shining, I believe in love even when I cannot feel it, I believe in God, even when he is silent.' So, even on our worst days, it cannot stop being true that God is on our side, that if we look at Jesus we see the nature of our Father, that if we look at the cross we see the extent of his love, that if we look at the empty tomb and the road to Emmaus we know that life is stronger than death, and that if we look at what happened at Pentecost we can know the power of his life in our own.

'I count everything loss', writes St Paul, 'compared with knowing Christ and the power of his resurrection.' But notice, he doesn't speak of 'having known Christ' but of 'knowing Christ' now. I sometimes find it odd to think that the day I got married was a day like any other. People dug their gardens and watched football and enjoyed the late autumn sunshine. But for me it was a turning point in my life: a day which has subtly affected every other day since. The day when 'I' became 'we'. And from then on every experience has been a shared experience. For our marriage isn't

13

a 'then' event – something that happened once many years ago. Our marriage is a 'now' event, something which has to be remade and entered into afresh each day. Of course there's a sense in which the resurrection of Jesus is a *then* event, something clearly fixed in history, experienced once on an ordinary day by a group of people who could no more deny it than they could deny they were alive. But the Church exists today because every Christian discovers that the resurrection is also a *now* event, not just something experienced in the past, nor something we hope for after we die. It's something we are to experience today: in this moment of time, a relationship with God in Christ who is alive for me and alive in me, as powerful now to open my blind eyes and unstop my deaf ears and set me free from the prison of my own making, and as it were raise me from the dead and give me new life. If I did not believe that to be true, if I had not found it to be true, I would have no right to speak to you. I know it is true; I know it as surely as I know the sun will rise tomorrow morning.

We are Easter people, people who live in the light of the resurrection. And we follow Jesus not because he makes us feel guilty but because he makes us glad. We don't ignore the reality of evil and the sin which eats into our lives. We see the negative and destructive things, but we see how they are met and transformed in the cross of Christ. The words we are called to live by are life-giving and life-enhancing words: peace, joy, forgiveness, victory and resurrection. Because of Easter we know that in the end all shall be well, and that we are held through life and through death by God who on Easter Day made it clear for all time how things truly are. May the joy of Easter and the power of the risen Christ be yours today and all through your lives.

4

Bread for the Starving and Water to the Parched

THIRD SUNDAY OF EASTER, 1983

Great St Mary's, Cambridge

I was brought up in the kind of church of which Bishop Joseph Butler would have approved when he remarked to John Wesley that 'enthusiasm in religion is a horrid thing, a very horrid thing'. Oh, it was dull. It was 'low', but in such a restrained way as to be without any compensating evangelical fervour, with Communion reluctantly added as a sort of 'afters' once a month at 12 noon; and sermons of inordinate length. How then do I come to be where I am?

Because by God's grace there later crossed my path two or three men who had the gift of communicating the love of God and the reality of Christ, and something of the meaning of his cross and the power of his risen life. What I didn't realise then, but have learned since, is that the Gospel where it is truly preached in terms of the love and forgiveness of God and the suffering and victory of Christ is like bread for the starving and water to the parched. And it never fails to win a response, for people have a great need and a great longing to hear that (whether they know it or not and whether they can accept it or not) they are understood and they are forgiven and they are loved by God.

In order to bring home first to the crowds and then to the disciples the life-giving nature of the Gospel, Jesus used bread. He took bread and shared it and fed them when the crowd by the lakeside, who had been so hungry for his words, then became physically hungry. He took bread and shared it in the Passover meal which was also the first Eucharist. After he was risen, it is in the breaking of bread that he is known at Emmaus. And it was as he took bread and shared it with them again at the lakeside that 'they knew it was the Lord'.

He had said of himself 'I AM the living bread, the bread which, if a man eats, he will never die'. Now, after Easter, they begin to understand what he means. Christ has fed them with the certainty of the Father's love and forgiveness, and he continues to feed them through death and into the new age which begins with his resurrection. Whoever believes in him and feeds on these truths will never be hungry again.

Every group of Christians needs constantly to remind itself of where its strength and distinctiveness lies. 'I must remind you', says Paul to the Church in Corinth, 'of the Gospel on which you have taken your stand and which is now bringing you salvation.' And then he spells it out: the belief that Jesus died for us on the cross; that he was raised to life and seen by many

17

witnesses; that death has been overcome; that neither death nor anything else has the power to separate us from the love of God. That is the Gospel we live for and many have died for; the resurrection faith we are to preach and to live in season and out of season.

The need in people to hear this Gospel remains constant, as insistent as hunger. Most human beings just aren't very good at making sense of the crazy paving of their lives. We're not good at coping with adversity, and not much better at coping with success. We search for answers, for peace of mind, for a sense of our own worth, a sense of joy and fulfilment. We need bread: why should we be fobbed off with junk food or pills?

Somehow we must learn to see – and help others to see – through the lens of the cross and the resurrection of Christ. And those of us who are given the daunting job of preaching this Gospel – actually seeking to communicate in words the mystery of the cross and the resurrection – must never forget what it is we are charged to do. We have to take the bread which is the word of God and break it and share it. It's very easy to get by with something less. To string words together which sound good but mean nothing and feed no one. For how do you dare stand up and speak of the power of God to change lives, or of dying in order to live, when you know you too often feel lost and battered and dispirited: that you too are one of the walking wounded?

You do it in fact because you know that, like John the Baptist, you don't point to yourself, nor speak simply out of your own limited experience: you point to the God who has grasped you and to truths which have been tested and proved by the Church of Christ down the centuries. *You speak of what you have received.* You speak of the suffering and death and resurrection of Jesus as they have been understood by Christians for 2,000 years: as an insight into the heart of God, and as an illumination of the way in which over and over again suffering has been used creatively and good brought out of evil. You point to the power of sacrificial love, now as then. You try not to say, 'Come and do what I do', but, 'Come and see what I see'. And while a few of us are charged to *preach* the Gospel of Christ crucified and risen, all of us are charged to *live* it. Which is why we place at our centre the Eucharist, which proclaims his health and at which we feed upon his life.

Where we fail to live the Gospel it is usually through fear. It is because all the time we are wanting to settle for something less, wanting a man-sized God and man-sized Gospel. It isn't that we simply can't believe in the Gospel of the cross and the resurrection and a God with the power to change us: it's that we dare not face what might happen if we did.

5

Mr Botha's Visit

GREAT ST MARY'S NEWSLETTER, JUNE 1984

Cambridge

This weekend, Mr P. W. Botha is in London. Clergy, Churchwardens and the Lay Chairman of the Parochial Church Council have written to Mrs Thatcher regretting this invitation, believing that it will be seen by the South African press as evidence that the British Government is not serious in its opposition to apartheid, and weaken the stand being taken by Christians and others within South Africa against their Government's policies.

In our letter to the Prime Minister (a copy of which may be seen in the office) we ask her to do three things:

- To leave Mr Botha in no doubt of our Government's disapproval of apartheid, and in particular to question him on the policy of resettling a further 1¾ million black people in barren 'Homelands';

- To press Mr Botha to make progress towards a just settlement in Namibia *within the framework* of UN Resolution 435, and not to renege from the formula for Namibian independence he has already in principle accepted; and

- Not to breach the spirit of the UN arms embargo to South Africa by selling their Government a number of British Aerospace BA748 reconnaissance planes as requested.

The spearhead for the opposition to government policy in South Africa is Bishop Desmond Tutu, General Secretary of the South African Council of Churches, whose courageous and ebullient witness to those fundamental truths of the Christian Gospel concerning men and women made in the image of God has caused his freedom to be curtailed and brought threats to his life.

Last year the World Council of Churches Assembly meeting in Vancouver expressed its admiration and support of the South African Council of Churches for its 'prophetic and courageous stand for human dignity, justice and liberation'; and three months ago it reaffirmed that support and commended the SACC to the prayers of all the churches when the South African Government Commission, set up to investigate the Council's activities, severely criticised that body and sought to dictate to the churches what the nature of Christian ministry should be.

Bishop Desmond Tutu's powerful refutation of the Commission's Report (a large part of which appeared in the *Guardian*) has made his position even more difficult. I wrote to him before Easter assuring him of our prayerful support, and I received this reply, dated Maundy Thursday:

> Just a quick word of thanks to you and your people for your love, caring and prayers. We are in splendid fettle. God is good and we have so many praying for and loving and supporting us. We can't lose. If God is for us who can be against us? Thank you all again. God bless you richly.

When Bishop Desmond's passport is restored to him, there is a standing invitation for him to preach at Great St Mary's. May that day soon come!

6

The Eighteenth Camel

12 JANUARY 1986

Great St Mary's, Cambridge

Before I was taken ill last June I didn't exactly claim to be indispensable. I just assumed that unless I was buzzing away at the centre of the hive things at Great St Mary's would rapidly start falling apart. Then along came this virus (myalgic encephalomyelitis). It would not be dictated to, counselled, exorcised, given a stewardship pledge – or even diagnosed. And so it was I who started rapidly falling apart.

Now for years I've known the Parable of the Eighteenth Camel, but in recent months I've begun to understand a bit more what it means. The tale of the eighteenth camel goes like this. A certain Arab had three sons. When he died, he left instructions in his will that his property should be divided up in a certain way. Everything was quite straightforward except for the camels, of which there were seventeen. The will said that half were to go to the eldest son, a third to the middle son, and a ninth to the youngest. Well, you just try dividing up seventeen camels by two, three

23

or nine, without ending up with a lot of amputated camels. So, finally, in desperation they went to a neighbour and asked his advice. The neighbour said: 'I have a camel. I will lend it to you and you will find that everything is resolved.' So he did, and, of course, once they had eighteen camels, it was very simple: the eldest son a half, that was nine, the second a third, that was six, and the youngest a ninth, that was two, making (and this is the point) seventeen camels in all. The neighbour then took his own camel back, and all was well.

That story contains a warning for those of us who are professional counsellors: therapists, doctors, priests, marriage counsellors, social workers, college tutors and the like. For it says that our role is not to become so much a part of someone's life that the one seeking help becomes dangerously and permanently dependent upon us. The danger is that you become for them an ideal substitute parent or husband or wife. Or even God. You become indispensable, and feeling yourself indispensable you become more and more frenetic. But that solves nothing, and those who counsel others must be like the   eighteenth camel, there to help people who face what seems an insoluble problem to look at it and work through it, and then gently, at the right time, to withdraw.

But the tale of the eighteenth camel has a wider application, for it's a story which actually illustrates one of the most profound of all Christian principles.

Let me put it like this. I am a Christian because I am convinced of certain truths about the nature of God and his plan for his creation. The heart of that plan is revealed at Christmas and Epiphany with the coming into the world of God's Son who brings new life and understanding to all who will receive it. This new life is quite simply to know and love God as our Father and each other as his children. And being a Christian, being the Church, means taking that truth so deeply into your heart and mind that it becomes part of our natural outlook. It means both learning how to live and helping others to discover how to live.

Now everywhere we look there are people for whom life seems an insoluble problem: people who feel puzzled and lost and unloved; people who are hungry for that simple knowledge of the love of God. And over and over again, in the darkness of people's lives, God invites us, his Church, to act as the eighteenth camel, to stand beside people and help them see life in a new light.

How? Not by imposing ourselves but by being there when we are needed. By giving time. By listening with care and attention. By proving trustworthy. By being ourselves. And by believing that God's grace can then in some extraordinary way use our tiny acts of love to point beyond ourselves to him as its source.

Behold the Lamb of God! In today's Gospel, John the Baptist – an eighteenth camel if ever there was one – points away from himself to the Christ. His whole life was spent in preparing for someone else, pointing men and women to a relationship and a life *he* could never give them. His success lay in making himself redundant.

And even Jesus points people away from himself. 'Don't cling to me,' he says to Mary Magdalene in the Easter garden. 'Don't focus on me, but through my words and my actions find your own way to my Father and your Father.'

In the end all human experience ought to be about finding our own way home to God, and all human relationships ought to be about helping each other to that end. For it is that deep inner conviction about the nature of God and his faithfulness, it is that trust, which enables us to live in the world with courage, and not only survive, but give thanks, both in times of illness and in health.

I don't yet know what we as a community may have learned from my long illness. But I know that I have learnt a bit and I hope am still learning, and that lesson number one is that vicars are no more indispensable to the community than anyone else. Take them away for a while and things don't fall apart. Eighteenth camels may be indispensable but there are plenty of them around. The grace of God works in surprising people in unexpected ways, and it's no bad thing to be stopped dead in your tracks at some point in your life, reminded of your frailty, and reduced to your proper size.

7

The Kingdom of God

PREACHED BEFORE THE CIVIC DIGNITARIES OF THE GREATER LONDON AREA, 7 SEPTEMBER 1986

Westminster Abbey

'However could you leave Cambridge', I was asked the other day, 'and come to live in London?' 'Because', I replied, 'London – noisy, polluted, traffic-clogged London – has always been, and will always be, a part of me, and once you have grown to love her she draws you back.' I came to London at the age of three, went to kindergarten in Regents Park, learnt to ride a bike on Primrose Hill and to swim in the Seymour Place Baths, and was only driven away by the war. Twenty years later I came back to London as a priest, for six years in Southwark, and for seven years at the BBC. I know London in all her moods, and though at times I long to escape from her, I love her dearly.

Now there is a word which I want to seize on and examine in terms of what ultimately *you* are about in your communities and what *we* are about in Westminster Abbey. It is the word 'vision'. As we read in the Book of Proverbs: 'Where there is no vision, the people perish.'

Vision is quite simply about *seeing*. In religious terms it means seeing the world as God's world. It means refusing to conform to the world's standards and values, or to go along with that cynical pessimism which some call realism but is in fact a terrible, destructive despair. To believe in God is to believe that there is a power for good in the world, a power that makes itself known in the deepest and most creative drives and forces in people and in nature; a power that in the last analysis is irresistible. To believe in God is to believe that in the end goodness will triumph over evil, justice over injustice, peace over war, that love will prove more powerful than violence, and that the compassionate service of others will prove more lasting than the gratification of oneself.

Vision in these terms is seen by the New Testament to mean a profound and revolutionary change in our understanding and in what we believe to be possible: a change in how we perceive the world, our neighbours and ourselves. It is as profound and as dramatic as the recovery of sight to one born blind, or the rebirth of one who is as good as dead. It has to do with faith and with hope; and it is at once utterly realistic and enormously costly. It is, in a word, what Jesus means by the Kingdom of God; and it is the vision for which he lived and died.

The Kingdom of God. It is not a phrase which exactly springs to mind or falls easily from our lips as we engage in our daily work, spend long hours on committees, do battle to improve civic life or seek to help those people who are damaged or deprived. And yet, if you were to come fresh to the four gospels and read them through from end to end, it would be the phrase that would strike you most forcibly: the Kingdom, God's Kingdom, which is to come 'on earth as it is in heaven'; the new community, the new ordering of society, the city – every city – as it might be.

It is, I repeat, the vision for which Jesus lived and died. For he, as a Jew, stands firmly in the tradition of the Old Testament prophets who made no distinction between what is sacred and what is secular, but saw that the worship of God and the right ordering of society go hand in hand. Loving God and loving your neighbour are the head and tails of a single coin. A penny, say, like the one with which they tested Jesus. And when he spoke of the things that belong to Caesar and the things that belong to God, he was saying nothing that conflicted with his whole teaching: that ultimately *everything* comes under the sovereignty of God and belongs to God. Did he not say to Pilate, when, with all the authority of the State, Pilate sought to judge him: 'You would have no authority over me unless it had been given from above'?

Jesus speaks again and again of the Kingdom of God. For him it is a reality which is at hand, coming to pass in small but significant ways wherever people are freed from sin and sickness and poverty, and begin to live as those who value each other because they know they are themselves of value to God. 'The Kingdom of God is *among* you.' He also speaks of it as something only to be fully realised in heaven, a reality beyond this world order, a vision of things to be hoped for.

Even as a child, Jesus has a passionate awareness both of God's nearness and his goodness, his fatherly care and compassion. No one knew the Father with the same trusting intimacy as he did, and his task is to lead others to the same source of power and love. He showed that all living souls, Jew, Gentile, Samaritan, rich Western industrialist, poor Bantu farm-worker, the ratepayers of Hampstead and Richmond as well as those of Wandsworth and Haringey, are ultimately created for the same kind of relationship with God that Jesus showed to be possible. For the vision of Jesus is to liberate human beings from those things which can imprison them: sickness of mind and body; injustice, racial discrimination; violence and the desire for revenge; the love of riches; the privilege of power.

Now I believe it is *our* job, at Westminster Abbey, to set before people this vision of a world transformed, this vision of a society of men and women whose perception of the sovereignty of God as well as his compassion enables them to begin to live together in love and peace. And I believe it is then *the* job of the civic dignitaries to help those in local boroughs to build the good society, to provide the poor with decent housing, food and clothing, the young with good schools, the sick with proper medical and community care and the elderly with a dignified old age. For wherever we free men and women from squalor or exploitation and enlarge their freedom to live full lives, then here is a sign of God's presence, a glimpse – a foretaste – of his Kingdom.

Yet those things, so good in themselves, cannot be achieved without the vision of the Kingdom of God and how it affects us. For man cannot live by bread alone, and Jesus demands of those who follow him a change at the level of spirit, that inward shift of vision and change of heart which is at once so necessary and so costly.

When he said that his Kingdom was 'not of this world', he was not saying it is entirely unworldly – just pie in the sky – but that it is not *worldly*, that its values are not the world's values. And in those radical, and really quite subversive, chapters in the gospels which we call the Sermon on the Mount, where he spells out the ethics of the Kingdom of God, he is inviting us to affirm, in our confused and complex society, certain permanent if unpopular values.

'Set your mind on God's Kingdom and his justice above everything else', he says.

That is to say:

Take your stand against a society obsessed by wealth and possessions. For in the Kingdom people are more concerned with giving than with having, with sharing than with possessing.

Take your stand against a society which values privilege and prestige so highly. For in the Kingdom

31

none is superior, none inferior; and the only privilege is that of serving others for their own sake. In the Kingdom each is cared for, loved and respected, not for what he *has* but for what he *is*: a valued child of God.

Take your stand against a society based on the narrow loyalties and prejudices of race, nationality, family, religious denomination or political party. For in the Kingdom the only solidarity that counts, and the only loyalty recognised, is the solidarity of the human race created in God's likeness. The hallmark of its members is not an exclusive self-interest but an all-embracing compassion.

And finally, *take your stand* against a society based on conflict which leads to recrimination, violence and revenge. For in the Kingdom you must first love your enemies, you must be reconciled, you must forgive and you must learn to accept forgiveness.

I said it was costly, this vision of the world as God's world, the people of our cities as God's people, our streets and homes and industries and offices as the place where truth and justice are to grow. It demands of us not only vision but integrity, imagination and (above all) that most lovely of qualities that springs from the heart, compassion. And yet we cannot duck the two imperatives laid on us, not simply in our private, but also in our public, lives, to love God and to love our neighbour.

At the very start of those three short years which were to have such a profound effect on the world, Jesus quoted words from the prophet Isaiah in his own local synagogue, words which encapsulated what he had come to do: 'to bring good news to the poor, to proclaim liberty to the captives, to set the down-trodden free'. But as soon as he began to spell out the implications of those works they would no longer listen and drove him from their midst. And when he persisted in challenging their assumptions with the radical new standards of God's Kingdom, they allowed him his title of 'King', wrote it on a board, and nailed both it and him to a cross. 'He claims to be King', they mocked, 'so let him reign from there.'

Westminster Abbey is a living witness to the fact that he does.

8

Unconditional, Fathomless, and Ours for the Asking

ADDRESS FOR A DAY OF PRAYER,
4 FEBRUARY 1989

Westminster Abbey

On the wall of my study I have hanging some beautiful words of the thirteenth-century German mystic, Meister Eckhart: 'Nothing in all creation is so like God as stillness.'

The truth is that it is when we come apart, and when we begin to learn the technique of stilling our restless minds and bodies, that we come close to God. That is not to say that God is ever far from us or that we can for one moment exist without his life-giving spirit informing and upholding us. It is rather that we become more aware, amid all the noise and distraction of our lives, that it is in him that we live and move and have our being. And that his nature and his name are love.

For there is no God other than the one revealed in the human likeness of Jesus Christ. All other gods are projections of ourselves: the fiercely judgemental god, the punitive and vindictive god, the god who makes us feel guilty, the god whom we can only approach if we use the right words and wear the right clothes and share the correct beliefs. For these are gods of our own creating.

For the God revealed by the man who told such simple, haunting stories, and healed the sick and forgave the sinful, and shared bread with the hungry and washed his followers' feet and hung upon a cross is a God whose nature and whose name cannot be anything else but Love, and who loves each of us with the kind of unconditional love which as yet we hardly begin to understand.

There is a sense in which the truths by which we are to live as Christians are at one and the same time profoundly mysterious (and we shall go on grappling with them all our lives), and yet also of a simplicity which a child can grasp. Indeed, Jesus said that if we are able to believe them in such a way that they become part of us and we begin to *live* them, then we will have rediscovered that childlike gift of taking what we are offered by those who love us on trust and responding with wonder. It is as we accept that we are loved – as a child holds out his hands to receive a gift, or accepts without questioning his parents' love – it is as we do this that we begin our journey towards God, that inner journey of prayer and worship and the proper love of yourself and your neighbour that is, and always has been, the story of the Christian life. A life which is uniquely mine as an individual *and* a life which we only experience properly in community.

Nothing helps us more on this pilgrimage of faith than to take certain profound truths and make them part of ourselves. Words of Jesus, or words of St Paul, or words of one of the Christian saints or mystics. To read such words, perhaps learn them, chew on them, keep silent with them in mind, to come back to them, repeat them, make them a part of our life, so that in times of darkness or temptation or doubt or sleeplessness or sickness or grief they can act as a kind of protective armour as well as a simple assertion of our trust in God.

For me, and for many, the words of Mother Julian of Norwich, the fourteenth-century mystic, are such words. In a few phrases they say it all. 'I desire to know what was Our Lord's meaning': that is to say, what was the meaning of his birth, his ministry, passion and death and rising again? And Julian was answered in inward understanding:

Would you know your Lord's meaning in this? Learn it well. Love was his meaning.

Who showed it to you? Love.
What did he show you? Love.
Why did he show you? For love.

Hold fast to this, and you shall learn and know more about love, than you will ever need to know or understand about anything else for ever and ever.

Love was his meaning. What is the meaning of love? Love is agape, the love defined by St Paul in the familiar thirteenth chapter of his first Letter to the Corinthians: 'Love is patient and kind ... never jealous ... never seeks its own advantage ... does not take offence or store up grievances ... it is always ready to make allowances, to trust, to hope and to endure whatever comes.' Love is the ability to put yourself in someone else's place: it is the accurate assessment and supply of someone else's need. It is not a soft emotional feeling: it is diamond-hard and costly, for it is a taking and breaking and sharing of yourself for the sake of others.

Jesus in his life and words and actions is the one who ultimately defines the meaning of love. For him it meant not only a boundless compassion for people, but a refusal to be moved from what he knew to be just and true and good, as well as a refusal to hate or to respond to violence and abuse with anything but an answering love. It can be, as it was for him, a kind of dying.

But where human love, even at its best and most costly and compassionate, always falls short of what it might be, the love of God is *unconditional* and *fathomless* – and it is ours for the asking.

That is the profound mystery plumbed by the Christian faith. That is the simple truth on which we are invited to base our lives.

Read once more these extraordinary words:

> Would you know our Lord's meaning in
> this? Learn it well. Love was his meaning.

> Who showed it to you? Love.
> What did he show you? Love.
> Why did he show you? For love.

> Hold fast to this, and you shall learn and
> know more about love, than you will
> ever need to know or understand about
> anything else for ever and ever.

9

God's Consoling Love

5 FEBRUARY 1989

Westminster Abbey

A former Archbishop of Canterbury, Michael Ramsey, used to tell the story of a mission service he went to as an undergraduate at an evangelical church in Cambridge. They sang a hymn of which the chorus consisted of the words 'almost persuaded'. Between each verse the missioner called dramatically on various people to leave the church: first, those who were unbelievers; then, those who had simply come to mock. And as a few students rose to go he flung out his arm with the damning phrase, 'Back to your women and your cigarettes!'

A far cry, you would think, from the one who sought the company of the despised tax gatherers like Levi and the sinners and outcasts with whom, according to this morning's gospel, he chose to sit and eat. Jesus did not denounce or condemn men and women for their sinfulness, but chose to mix with them and share their meals. And some were amazed and some were scandalised. But if his behaviour was scandalous to the rich and the comfortable and to the religious leaders, it was for the poor, the sinful and those that the church had condemned a source of joy and healing.

It was not that he sat lightly to their messy lives. It was rather his way of making them understand that however far they had strayed from God, however tangled and spoiled their lives might be, they were not cut off from God and his great love for them: that the moment we truly *want* God, we have him; the moment we truly say 'I am sorry', we can know the joy of forgiveness – both human and divine.

What seems to have angered Jesus most of all was the assumption on the part of some that they had no need of forgiveness; and indeed, he went so far as to say that only if we have our eyes opened to our deep and constant need to be forgiven can we hear his word or claim to be his follower. Why did he come? Why was he born? Why did he so anger the powers that be that they crucified him? 'I came', said Jesus, 'to call sinners to repentance.' 'I came that those who are blind' – and which of us is not? – 'might see.'

In the language that Jesus spoke, Aramaic, the word for 'sin' really means 'a debt'. 'Forgive us our debts.' Forgive us all the claims on our love we have failed to meet. Forgive us for every refusal to give ourselves to others; and forgive the hurts, known and unknown, we inflict one upon another.

You know, we get it wrong, we misunderstand this Christian faith of ours time and time again. For the Gospel is *not* about keeping some set of rules, or about living respectable lives, or about denying our real feelings or pretending to be other than we are. The Gospel is about God revealed in a man who healed the sick and forgave the sinner, and who brought joy to the bewildered, the damaged and the sinful (and none of us is excluded from that list) because he lived and died, loved and taught, to make clear once and for all time the certainty of God's consoling love for every single one of his creatures.

And we Christians don't claim to be better than anyone else; simply more aware of what we are and more conscious of our need of God. Nor do we claim to be different from other people, except perhaps in one respect: that we have the experience whenever we wish of being forgiven, of having our debt wiped out, of being set free from the errors of the past; and of having to do with a God who knows us and sees us not simply as we are, but as by his grace we shall be.

10

Uncalculating, Indiscriminate, Unconditional Love

25 FEBRUARY 1990

Westminster Abbey

The charge? Adultery.

The evidence? Caught in the act.

The sentence? Stoning to death.

The judge? Jesus.

In John 8:1–11, we see most perfectly expressed the quality which drew people to Jesus and has drawn them ever since: a mixture of blazing, uncompromising truth and tender compassion. He does not condemn, nor does he condone. He does not judge the woman, but neither does he dismiss her. He simply invites her to see in him the love of God for what it is, and in so doing to be changed and set free by that small miracle we call forgiveness.

Look at the scene again. It's the priests, the religious leaders, who drag the woman before Jesus in order to test him and see how he responds. They want proof that he is a blasphemer and a heretic as they suspect. Here is the heart of a conflict which is with us still – the conflict between the law and the Gospel, justice and mercy.

The law of Moses demands she must be stoned. The Gospel says she may be forgiven. Jesus accepts there is a need for law, for without it there would be moral and social anarchy; but he rejects the system which the Pharisees represent, whereby you earn or lose merit in the sight of God by living your life according to a set of *inflexible* rules and principles, for that makes nonsense of the whole concept of God's freely given grace. And it is this grace that is the heart of Jesus' teaching which to many has always been puzzling, if not shocking: this fact of God's uncalculating, indiscriminate and unconditional love. He illustrates it in parables like that of the labourers in the vineyard, where the last to be hired is treated every bit as generously as the first, or in that of the Prodigal Son, where the returning Prodigal is welcomed without question and with open arms, to the fury of his elder brother who has stayed at home.

There are no rules, then, which if we observe them we stand right with God: there is only his generosity. There are no conditions, only his love. All are sinners: all may be forgiven. 'Let him who is without sin throw the first stone', says Jesus. And those who have

43

dragged this woman before him know they too stand convicted and they go out one by one: 'the eldest first', you note, for even in defeat the Pharisees keep the correct order of precedence. And Jesus says, revealing in this moment the eternal nature of the God he has come to make known: 'Has no one condemned you? Neither do I condemn you. Go in peace and do not sin again.'

It is a simple, uncomplicated story, yet at the heart of it there lies a life-changing truth. Jesus is not saying to the woman that her adultery doesn't matter. Of course it matters. It's an offence against love. But neither does he play on her guilt or her fear. He simply assures her that, whatever she has done and for whatever reason, she is not thereby cut off from the love of God. The moment we *want* God, we have him; the moment we turn to him recognising our sinfulness we are met by his love and forgiveness.

This is what the Christian Gospel is about. It is not about keeping some set of rules, or about denying our real feelings or pretending to be other than we are. It's about responding to a God who is revealed in the words and actions of this man who brought joy to the poor, the damaged and the sinful because he lived and died to convince them of the certainty of God's unconditional love for each of us, his creatures, and our value in his sight. And it is this truth, above all others, which the Church is in the business of proclaiming.

A highly impressive Lutheran pastor from East Berlin, Chairman in that city of that body of people from all political parties who are responsible for bringing their fellow citizens out of the years of repression into democracy, described how Mr Honeker, the former East German leader, now reviled and abused for his regime and seriously ill with cancer, has found sanctuary only in the churches, for they are taking seriously Jesus' command that we should love our enemies.

'Has no man condemned you? Neither do I condemn you. Go in peace and do not sin again.' In those few words we see the transforming quality of the love of God in Christ. This is why they were drawn to him. And only when the Church and we its members know at first hand that we constantly need to ask forgiveness of God and of one another and be absolved, and in our turn to forgive others – only then shall we convey truly the heart of the Christian Gospel. Only in this way are we set free of the crippling chains of the past to respond with tentative but increasing joy to the unchanging compassion of God.

11

Whatever You Do, I Love You

30 JUNE 1991

Westminster Abbey

Under the heading 'Whose Child are You?' a Sunday paper asked a dozen people, 'Tell us, who was the special person in your childhood who made you what you are: your mother, your father – or someone else?' One man wrote in reply: 'Undoubtedly my mother. She has great honesty and unquestioning love. She never interferes but is always there when I need her. Hers is the purest form of parental love: Whatever you do, I love you. You are my son.'

'Tell us, how does God view sinners?' the Pharisees ask Jesus, shocked by the company he keeps. And in reply he tells perhaps the most powerful of all his stories: the story of the lost son. 'If you would know the heart of God,' he says in effect, 'you must ask yourselves what a parent feels when a child who has been lost to them returns home.'

Nothing touches the nerve of what it means to be a Christian more powerfully than the end of this story in which God's love is declared in the father's running to meet and embrace his returning child. In the words I quoted just now: 'Whatever you do, I love you. You are my son.'

That's the story which can be universally understood. It was an Indian preacher who once suggested that the moment at which the Prodigal Son really repented was when he reached home and saw that in his absence his father's hair had turned white. For of course this story isn't just a masterly insight into the meaning of forgiveness – it's also the definitive story of what it means to love. Of what it can *cost* to love, in this case for a parent to love unconditionally and without limit. 'Whatever you do, I love you. You're my son, my daughter, my child.' Jesus' story says that at the heart of all true loving, divine and human, there is pain and loss, but that there is a love which will outlast everything and that cannot be destroyed, for it is of God and, whether we know it or not, we live constantly under its shadow. What God is saying in Jesus Christ is, 'You are loved'. But it is up to us to return home to the place where our Father waits – the one who, when he sees us coming, runs to meet us.

Or does he? A few years ago I went to see the Royal Ballet perform their version of the story of the Prodigal Son. In the final scene the boy comes home starving, filthy and ashamed. His father, standing on the far side of the stage, sees his son at the same instant as his son sees him. At once he instinctively stretches out his arms in welcome but he makes no other movement. Then his arms drop to his side and he waits as the boy, painfully slowly, drags himself across the stage to him. As the boy does so, and as he clutches at his feet and then his robe, the father stiffens, his hands clench and unclench, but he still makes no move. And so the boy pulls himself up until he is hanging curled like a small child again on his father's breast. And only then does his father, in an action of infinite tenderness, enfold him in his great cloak and carry him from the stage.

Curtain. And it's a moving and thoughtful variation of the way Jesus tells the story. And not untrue to that other aspect of God's love we sometimes ignore – his justice. The Old Testament often pictures a God who is ambivalent about his creation – sometimes angry, impatient at human foolishness and slowness to understand him, grieved by our sin and our lack of response, yet at the same time infinitely tender and compassionate. You find the same ambivalence in Jesus. He can be angry at people's blindness, impatient with the Pharisees, urgent in calling people to repent, to open their eyes and see, yet at the same time there is a luminous compassion and gentleness in dealing with individuals in their hurt and isolation.

So here are two truths in tension. The first is that God's love for me is unconditional: the second that God is unable to make me experience that love, that forgiveness, unless I come to understand my need and respond with the words: 'Father, I have sinned. I want to come home.'

It is as if God's love is like a wind that can only blow in one direction: it blows, this wind, this Holy

Spirit, towards fullness of life, towards wholeness, and it wants to take us with it, so that those who, in the words of today's epistle, are compassionate, kind, gentle and loving, forgiving and thankful, part of God's new creation, are those who have turned round and have the wind at their backs; but those who remain enclosed and isolated within themselves, unloving, perhaps embittered by life, are those who are still battling against the wind. It's not that God's love for them is any the less – any more than the father's love for his son was diminished when he was living it up in a country far from home – but if we choose to work against the grain of God then we can't experience him as love, for then everything seems to be against us – even God.

I have thought a lot about that still figure in the ballet of the Prodigal Son, waiting without movement while his son slowly crawls towards him, waiting without movement while he climbs into his arms and only then embracing him. It well suggests the anguish in the heart of God as his justice wrestles with his mercy, and the depths to which the Father is hurt by the way we spoil our lives. It shows what it costs the Father to go on loving and the son to say he is sorry; and it shows our need to become a child again if we are to hear those words: 'Whatever you do, I love you. You're my child.'

Yet in the end it's the other version, the one that Jesus tells, which has the greater power to win us back to God, where, 'while he was yet a long way off, his father saw him and had compassion, and ran and embraced him and kissed him'. For it is that keeping watch and joyful recognition and running to meet us and embracing us which more than anything else bring home to us the unconditional nature and the sheer prodigality of our Father's love. And how, then, having seen that in Jesus, can we not respond?

12

Anger

There was once a king of whom it was said that when he was angry one of his eyes became so fearsome that those on whom he looked fainted on the spot, or even expired. The only thing that kept his anger in check was his fear of decimating his kingdom.

There is anger in each one of us. Sometimes it's close to the surface; more often it's buried so deep that, if and when it emerges – as it may, for example, when we are seriously bereaved – it takes us by surprise. Yet anger is something we are born with, part of our make-up, and there is nothing more spectacularly angry than a raging and frustrated baby. One of its more fashionable forms today is road rage, when it erupts in a way quite disproportionate to the incident that triggers it. And that sort of anger is easily recognised for what it is: cheap anger, easy-to-come-by anger, a self-indulgent anger because we are thwarted or put down or (though we won't admit it) simply in the wrong: a bad-tempered letting off of steam that can damage both ourselves and others. The child in us throwing our toys around. And that is the anger that is listed among the seven deadly sins.

Yet it is not quite so simple: nothing about human beings ever is. For it is now widely recognised that depression hides a deep-seated anger, and it was Freud who spotted in his depressed patients that the anger they might have hurled against others or their environment or God they had in fact directed against themselves. But the anger is usually buried so deep that it is not recognized as such, and the depressed person is the last to admit to being angry. If you can release the anger, said Freud, the depression will begin to lift.

Why should we fear and repress our anger? Because as children we're taught to control our emotions, taught that anger and feelings of aggression are destructive and need to be bottled up; and in many families – especially British families – the expression of strong feelings, especially negative feelings, is discouraged, thought to be in rather bad taste. With the result that very natural feelings of anger and resentment that are part of most people's make-up are then driven deep underground.

So how do we cope with this un-discharged rage? By recognising it and admitting it; perhaps by giving vent to it and so letting it go. William Blake shows great psychological insight when he writes:

I was angry with my friend,
I told my wrath, my wrath did end.
I was angry with my foe,
I told him not, my wrath did grow.

You'll find a great deal of anger in the Bible, most of it directed against God. And naturally so. For if God has given us life, and if God is all-powerful, and if life is so manifestly unfair and so full of things that may hurt us and cause us pain, is it not right to rail against him? The Psalms do so: they are full of angry questions. The prophets do so: they can be angry when God seems to have deserted them. There is the despairing anger of Job: 'I will speak out in the distress of my mind and complain in the bitterness of my soul. Why have I become thy target?' And there's Jonah, who complains bitterly when even the gourd giving him some shade from the blazing sun begins to wither and God summons up a scorching wind. And he's furious. And God says: 'Are you right to be angry?' 'Yes', replies Jonah, 'mortally angry!'

We should always be honest with God, and there's nothing wrong or strange about being angry with him. 'A god whom we can easily bear', writes Paul Tillich, 'a god whom we do not hate in moments, a god whose destruction we never desire, is not [the true] God at all, and has no reality.' When Martin Luther told his confessor that he couldn't pray, he was told it was not because God was angry with him, but because he was angry with God and must learn to tell him so. And

Luther comments: 'This was magnificently said.' And there may well be times when we need to tell God how hurt we are, how let down, how angry.

One of the angriest, most moving poems in the language is *The Collar* by George Herbert. It begins:

> I struck the board, and cry'd, No more.
>   I will abroad.
> What? Shall I ever sigh and pine?
> My lines and life are free; free as the rode
> Loose as the winde, as large as store.
>   Shall I be still in suit?

Herbert could only find his answer in those words of St Paul: 'Were you not as Christians taught the truth as it is in Jesus?' For the Christian claim is that in Christ the true nature of God is revealed, and that in the Cross of Christ God willingly opens himself to the worst that human rage can do without any diminishing of his love. Let me give you an illustration of what I mean.

There is a moving novel by the American writer Peter de Vries called *The Blood of the Lamb*. It's about a father whose eleven-year old child is dying of leukaemia, and it is a perceptive mixture of humour, pain and rage. He can't forgive God for his daughter's illness, and sometimes he gives way to his anger and despair:

> He wandered out into the garden in the
> cool of the evening awaiting the coming

of the Lord. No such advent taking place, he shook his fist at the sky and cried, 'If you won't save her from pain, at least let me keep her from fear!' A brown thrush began his evening note, the ever favoured, unendurable woodsong. He snatched up a rock from the ground and stoned it from the tree.

Later he wonders how the other parents in the children's ward can chatter of this and that but never speak of the anger and hurt that burn within them.

Rage and despair are indeed carried about in the heart, but privately, to be let out on special occasions, like savage dogs for exercise, occasions in solitude when God is cursed, birds stoned from the trees or the pillow hammered in darkness.

On his daughter's birthday he takes a beautiful iced cake to the hospital but learns on his arrival that she has just died. There follows a great bursting anger against God. He goes to a nearby church still clutching the birthday cake and throws it with all his strength at the crucifix standing outside.

It was miracle enough that the pastry should reach his target at all ... the more

so that it should land square, just beneath
the crown of thorns. Then through scalded
eyes he seemed to see the hands free
themselves of the nails and move slowly
towards the soiled face. Very slowly, but
very deliberately, with infinite patience,
the icing was wiped from the eyes and flung
away.

At Calvary God in Christ invites us to vent our anger
upon him in order that we may discover in him
a forgiveness, an understanding and a love that is
infinitely stronger than our hate. And George Herbert's
poem, after a torrent of increasingly angry words, ends:

> But as I rav'd and grew more fierce
> and wilde
> At every word,
> Me thoughts I heard one calling, *Childe*:
> And I reply'd, *My Lord*.

To stop there would be to tell only half the story, but I
will only paint the other face of anger in the broadest
strokes. For the Bible is also full of the anger of God,
an anger born of compassion and a concern for justice.
It is a wholly righteous anger directed against all that
spoils his creation and works to prevent the coming
of his Kingdom. It is the anger of the prophets at the
exploitation of the poor. It is the anger of Jesus when

he drives the moneychangers out of the Temple, or is faced with the blindness of the Pharisees. Yet God's anger is always more than matched by his compassion. God's anger is no expression of temper, but an anger that we his children can be so blind and deaf and perverse, so ready to exploit others, so constantly falling short of what we are created to be.

Do we feel that kind of anger? Please God, we do. Anger about poverty or homelessness or racism or the arms trade or the market in drugs, for if that kind of anger provokes us to protest and to take action, then it is the very opposite of self-indulgence: indeed, it is our saving grace. It is a sign that we are made in the image of the God who has set before us the very different standards of his Kingdom. May it be that he demands of us not less, but *more* of his kind of anger? The anger born of compassion and a desire for justice? Yes, I think it may.

Lord God, my heavenly Father, you know the secrets of my heart. Forgive me my self-indulgent anger by which I can hurt others and myself. Give me insight into the unresolved tensions in my life, that I may be free to express my true feelings in your presence. Help me to recognise every injustice and every form of evil that is destructive of your Kingdom, and share in that divine anger that is an expression of your love. I ask this for the sake of Jesus Christ, our Lord. Amen.

13

Remember

16 FEBRUARY 1997

Southwark Cathedral

The LORD God formed a human being from the dust of the ground and breathed into his nostrils the breath of life, so that he became a living creature. (Genesis 2:7)

Then their eyes were opened, and they knew that they were naked. (Genesis 3:7)

There stands on the pavement outside the west front of Westminster Abbey a unique memorial. It was unveiled by the Queen in the presence of representatives of innocent victims of war and violence from many parts of the world: not the members of the armed services who have died in war, but millions of men, women and children who have happened to be in the way when the dogs of war, or evil and destructive passions, have been let loose among them. *Remember*, it says in stark letters across the centre of the circular stone – *Remember all innocent victims of oppression, violence and war.* And around the edge, catching the eye of everyone who walks into the Abbey, *Is it nothing to you all you who pass by?*

The Jewish woman who came to that unveiling ceremony to represent the Jewish victims of the Holocaust had been, like Anne Frank, first in Auschwitz, then in Belsen. She may well have seen the fifteen-year-old girl with dimpled cheeks and great dark eyes who was to die in Belsen just weeks before its liberation, a girl whose words were almost miraculously preserved, and have touched the hearts of millions.

And if we ask why, if we ask what gives her diary the power still to speak so powerfully to us, I believe the answer lies in the word 'humanity'. For it is a revealing record of a child journeying through puberty, that journey from a state of dependence to one of independence in the most extraordinary circumstances, and in the privacy of her diary illustrating the heights and the depths of which human beings made in the image of God are capable: on the one hand, the courage and the hope, and on the other, the pettiness, the squabbling and the selfishness. She holds nothing back, admitting her own nakedness, that is to say, her vulnerability, and irritated beyond measure by the behaviour of the seven others confined with her in that attic annexe.

'Why do grown-ups quarrel so easily,' she asks, 'and over the most idiotic things? Mrs van Daan's grizzling is unbearable ... she nags us the whole day. It really would be nice to dump her in a bucket of cold water and put her up in the loft.' Dr Dussel the dentist is a stodgy, old-fashioned disciplinarian and preacher of long-drawn-out sermons on manners, refusing to give way over the most trivial of matters, ungrateful that they have given him shelter. Anne quotes Goethe: 'The spirit of a man is great. How puny are his deeds!' She even finds her adored father insensitive, and is distressed by her seemingly unmaternal mother: 'Just had a big bust-up with Mummy for the umpteenth time. I don't pronounce judgment of her character, for that is something I can't judge, but I look at her as a mother and she just doesn't succeed in being that to me. She seems to push me away.' Even Peter, the van Daan's son, on whom she comes to depend more and more in an intimate and loving friendship, distresses her in the end by refusing to share with her his most private self. But through these two years Anne herself is growing in self-knowledge, and in that necessary awareness of the complexity of other people, which in our childish innocence we don't at first suspect or begin to understand. So from the 1944 diary we read:

> Why is it that people always try so hard to hide their real feelings? Why do we trust each other so little? It seems as if I've grown up a lot ... even my attitude towards the van Daans has changed. I suddenly see all the arguments ... in a different light. I hope that I've acquired a bit of insight and will use it well .... I came across letters (from

1942) dealing with Mummy ... I was quite shocked and wondered how I could have been so brimful of rage and filled with hate ... I have been trying to understand the Anne of a year ago and to excuse her.

This self-analysis is to feature more and more in the final months of the diary. In November 1942 she had written that she 'feels more and more like a song-bird whose wings have been brutally clipped and who is beating (herself) in utter darkness against the bars of the cage ... I go to lie on the divan and sleep to make the time pass more quickly, and the stillness and the terrible fear, because there is no way of killing them.' She is either on top of the world or in the depths of despair; now in May 1944 she can still write that she feels utterly broken 'from the bad food, the strain, the miserable atmosphere, my disappointment in Peter', and yet she can be lifted out of it by an unexpected gift of flowers, a Whitsun cake from their friend Miep, or by a glimpse of the night sky through an open window: 'When I look up at the sky, the clouds, the moon and the stars make me calm and patient ... prepared to face every blow courageously.'

Anne writes, in the last entry of all:

I have one outstanding trait in my character ... my knowledge of myself ... The Anne of every day I can face entirely without prejudice, without making excuses

61

for her, and watch what's good and what's bad about her. I understand more and more how true Daddy's words were when he said: 'All children must look after their own upbringing.' Parents can only give good advice or put them on the right paths, but the final forming of a person's character lies in his own hands.

And again:

I am a little bundle of contradictions: I know exactly how I'd like to be, how I am too ... inside. But, alas, I'm only like that for myself (when alone). I try terribly hard to change myself, but I'm always fighting against a more powerful enemy – so that the bad is on the outside and the good is on the inside, and I keep on trying to find a way of becoming what I would so like to be, and what I could be ... if there weren't any other people living in the world.

And that is how her diary ends, three days before the Nazis break into their hiding-place. No 'saint', then, this Anne Frank, but like us all in the vulnerability of our humanity, a mixture of good and bad, courageous and cowardly, self-giving and selfish. A fifteen-year-old brought to an unusually mature state of self-knowledge so that we see her with all the pretences down, naked in the garden in her vulnerability, yet one made in the likeness of God for an eternal destiny.

And so I come back to the innocent victims and their remembering. For what that stone at the Abbey is witnessing to is the infinite value of every man, woman and child made in the image of God; *and* to the capacity for evil and destruction that lies in all our hearts; *and* to the redemptive power of good that is seen in every act of self-giving love or courage or generosity, and that undying hope that remains unquenched even in the darkest of times.

But truly to *remember* Anne Frank and those like her is not just to recall them to mind. It is to do something infinitely more creative. It is to ask that God in his love and mercy will re-member them, re-member those who have been dis-membered: recreate them, refashion them in his own likeness, as in his good and loving purpose he has always intended them ultimately to be.

This, after all, is what we are asking for ourselves at every Eucharist: we are asking God to re-member us, to recreate us, to refashion us in the likeness of the body of Christ, so that we may be open to the Father, whatever life, with all its unpredictability, may do to us, and open to each other in that new creation made possible by the death and resurrection of Jesus.

Some may protest that Anne was Jewish. I would reply that the God revealed by Jesus Christ, the God who is the Father of us all, the God who chose himself in Christ to enter into our suffering, is the God whose nature and name are Love. And his purpose for

Anne, for her parents, for Peter and the van Daans and tiresome Dr Dussel, with all their deeply human failings, is not to be thwarted by an untimely death. They, like us all, are made in God's image. Which is why, like the penitent thief hanging beside Jesus on a cross, we can pray: 'Lord, remember them, re-member them, when you come into your Kingdom.'

14

Word Become World

ANNUAL SHAKESPEARE SERMON, 26 APRIL 1998

Holy Trinity Parish, Stratford

'Words, words, mere words,' says Shakespeare's Troilus, 'no matter from the heart.' I would above all else speak from the heart.

My own Shakespeare story begins as a schoolboy in the last years of the war in the unlikely setting of the Pavilion Theatre, Torquay, home each summer to concert parties: Clarkson Rose's *Twinkle* and the *Fol-de-Rols*. But when autumn came there arrived – like some actor-manager from a previous age – Donald Wolfit. I saw him as Lear, Othello, Shylock, Macbeth and Malvolio, and it was a revelation. In retrospect I realised that the productions were a travesty, the company mainly feeble satellites orbiting the central star; and Wolfit's curtain-calls – drained, exhausted, one hand clutching the stage curtain – are never to be forgotten. But then neither is the sheer energy and authority of a handful of performances that for me and for many unlocked the magic door into the world of Shakespeare.

When in those same years the undergraduate Bernard Levin saw the Hamlet of Donald Wolfit (who used to bring the curtain down at the line 'and flights of angels sing thee to thy rest' lest he should not be centre-stage to the last), Levin wrote that the genius of Shakespeare revealed to him that night was:

> of a beauty, vigour, humanity, wisdom, wit, imagination, maturity, grace, feeling, profundity, richness and understanding that embraced all the qualities of everything of all the authors I had ever read put together, and a very great deal more besides.

At school I was to play Prince Hal and Hamlet, which convinced me that the stage was the only possible career (God, as so often, had other ideas). Then in 1948 I came to Stratford and saw Godfrey Tearle and Diana Wynyard in *Othello*, and Robert Helpman as a somewhat camp King John; and *The Winter's Tale*, with Scofield playing the old shepherd's son, Clown.

There is, of course, a clowning side to Stratford that would no doubt have appalled and fascinated Shakespeare in equal measure. William Golding picked it up in an essay forty years ago:

> You can buy that broad, bald head, that
> fattening face and pointed beard, attached
> to almost anything … You can use him as
> a paperweight, as the handle of a bell or a
> shoehorn … You can stir your coffee or poke
> your fire with him. You can use him as a
> brush to sweep dust into him as a shovel …
> He looks with an awful fixity out of certain
> shops – as well he might, because now he is
> a milk jug, the top of his head pried open,
> while the handle sticks out of one ear and
> the spout out of the other.

Nearly fifty years after my first memorable visit I came back to Stratford for an even more memorable one. Shakespeare had never been far from my thoughts, for every weekday morning for ten years my day began in Westminster Abbey in the small chapel of St Faith, which stands at the far end of Poets' Corner, and I would pass William Kent's fine eighteenth-century monument of him and give him a glancing look of gratitude. And it was in part of my Deanery, that historic room known as the Jerusalem Chamber, that Shakespeare (accurately) sets the death of King Henry IV. And then two years ago a friend told me that Peter Hall, for his production of *Julius Caesar*, had insisted on a large crowd of extras and that they were using amateurs for the first time in years. He was one of them. Knowing that I had acted in Peter Hall's first productions when we were fellow-undergraduates at

Cambridge, he asked if I would like to be a 'fill-in' extra at a Saturday matinee. So one Saturday in December I came here and played a Roman senator, a citizen and a soldier. It was a particularly blood-filled production, and after the murder of Caesar we all escaped into the narrow trench that runs under the front of the Stratford stage. As the conspirators filed past us in the confined space, their daggers dripping with blood, I thought that choral evensong would just be starting at the Abbey and wished that my colleagues could see me.

Now you cannot be fully seized by the invasive power of Shakespeare until you see the plays in the theatre. Will Shakespeare was an actor: he wrote for actors; he knew in his bones how an actor functions, knew the feel of holding an audience in the palm of your hand and working that magic that only the theatre provides. In his book, *The Empty Stage*, Peter Brook writes of what he calls 'the Holy Theatre', or the theatre of the 'invisible-made-visible', and we know what he means: a performance, say, of *Lear* or *Othello*, that transcends our daily experience, fires the spirit and enables us to glimpse the face of the invisible which is at once both familiar and mysterious. Familiar, because we may recognise aspects of ourselves in Hamlet, Hermione or Angelo; but also mysterious, an awareness of that indefinable beyondness-at-the-heart-of-things that can take your breath away. Somewhere inside us a resonance is stirred about what it means to be human, with all our needs, all our capacity for good and evil, all our potential for revenge or for mercy, cruelty or compassion; and we may know brief moments when the world is transfigured. Moments when, to echo Lear's words to the dead Cordelia, we:

> Take upon's the mystery of things,
> As if we were God's spies.

It was T. S. Eliot who said that all great literature is our contemporary, transcending its own time and place by the timeless quality of its language and the timeless nature of its concerns; and Joseph Conrad wrote of how 'the artist speaks to the sense of mystery surrounding our lives: to our sense of pity, and beauty and pain'.

Shakespeare's words and characters, his content, is eternally valid because each new generation can say: 'It is valid for us; it speaks, as all great art does, of what a human being is and what a human being could be.'

So what is it that sets Shakespeare apart from all other poets and playwrights? It is, of course, the extraordinary breadth of his vision. In those global plays written for, and performed in, the Globe all of the world *was* his stage. In telling his stories, in his probing of character and motive, Shakespeare captures in words all that is deepest and most strange within us and so tells our story too. Not only does he have this unique understanding of the human heart and its inner motives and depths, its potential for greatness and its predilection for evil, but he also explores the wider world and sets our desires, hopes and ambitions against the marvellously rich tapestry of the English Court or the battlefield at Agincourt, the walls of Troy or the sea coast of Bohemia, the Venetian Rialto or the streets of Verona, the Senate in Rome or the Forest of Arden.

A second reason for Shakespeare's uniqueness is his ability to juggle 'the mystery of things' with the nitty-gritty of life in all its grubby detail. Peter Brook writes:

> His aim continually is holy, metaphysical, yet he never makes the mistake of staying too long on the highest plane. He knew how hard it is for us to keep company with the absolute – so he continually bumps us down to earth ... We have to accept that we can never see all of the invisible. So after straining towards it, we have to face defeat, drop down to earth, then start up again.

What other writer has combined so successfully a sense of the numinous, the mystery of the world and our place within it, and our humanity, both its Godlikeness and its absurdity? Hamlet and Aguecheek, Bottom and Cleopatra, Prospero and Dogberry and Lancelot Gobbo.

But it is something else that captivates us in the end: it's the power of his language, the music of his poetry. Others have written powerful plays about doomed heroes who show a self-confident contempt for a divine moral order and their proper place within it, and demonstrate the flaw of *hubris*, the sight of whose punishment arouses in us a healthy pity and terror, that purging of strong emotion known as *catharsis*. Others have taken the a and the b and the c of the alphabet, Eliot's 'slimy mud of words' and 'approximate thoughts and feelings' and moulded them into a language that tugs at the heart, illuminating the familiar in unforgettable words. Is it not a matter for wonder how the greatest plays and novels and poetry, the wisdom of philosophers and the holiness of the saints, have all reached us dressed in the 26 letters of the alphabet and the words they form, from that first bedtime story we hear at our mother's knee to – well, by some strange and wondrous alchemy, to *Anna Karenina* and *Paradise Lost* and *The Sonnets of Shakespeare* and *The Tempest*? Yet it is Shakespeare who is unique in combining the force of a mind of quite exceptional understanding and creativity with an ear for – oh, for:

> 'Good shepherd, tell this youth what 'tis
> to love'
> 'There is a willow grows aslant a brook'
> 'Make me a willow cabin at your gate'
> 'Go, bind thou up yon dangling apricocks'
> 'We two alone will sing like birds i'
> the cage'
> 'Farewell, a long farewell, to all my
> greatness!'
> 'Men must endure

Their going hence, even as their
    coming hither.
Ripeness is all.'

But it is not just the music of the words that sends
us spinning. It's something more profound. I said at
the start that I would speak from the heart, for only
words that come from my centre can hope to speak
to yours. My desire is not just to string words together
in the best order, but to give you my word, to give
you something that is part of me. When Shakespeare
gives us his word, he – like every great writer – speaks
out of his own centre. Of course he speaks as a man
of his own time, and against a background of its own
turbulent history. Yet he is both circumscribed and
liberated by his Stratford grammar school education.
For he has something which the latter could not give
him: the skill of what Anthony Burgess calls 'putting
words together in new and surprising patterns which,
miraculously, reflect some previously un-guessed truth
about life'. Somehow, by his words, the familiar world
is transfigured.

The poet Seamus Heaney, writing of his childhood
and youth, describes the unforgettable moment when
he first read the work of another Irish poet, Patrick
Kavanagh. Of how Kavanagh:

Took my familiar world and embodied it,
enfleshed it, in new-minted words. [Here
was] the strange stillness and heat and

solitude of the sunlit fields, the inexplicable melancholy of distant work-sounds, in a language that was familiar yet strangely new … All at once I knew the primitive delight in finding world become word.

'World become word.' We honour Shakespeare because he too took our familiar world and 'embodied it, enfleshed it, in new-minted words', words which came from the heart.

Now, if I say, 'I give you my word', I mean that phrase in two senses. I mean I have struggled to take something that lies at my own centre, something that makes me *me*, and share it with you. In offering you 'my word' I offer you something of myself. The second, more obvious, meaning of 'I give you my word' is 'You can trust me. I give you my word, my word of honour.' And though Falstaff would dismiss the concept of honour as a mere word, nothing more than air, words and breath are all we have if our invisible thoughts and ideas are to be incarnated, given substance, breath become speech, all we have with which to pass the time of day or make a declaration of love, or even share an insight about the Mystery.

Now if it is true that at our best and truest we communicate with each other by revealing something of our own inner being, that is to say, by giving our word, then it must be true of the God in whose image we are made. So Genesis tells of a God who speaks out of a profound silence and says: 'Let there be light!' And as chaos gives way to order, the morning stars sing together and all the Sons of God shout for joy because time has begun, a story has begun. And over aeons of time God (like a writer or an artist does) sings his creation into being, sings into being banks:

> Whereon the wild thyme blows,
> Where oxlips and the nodding
>   violet grows
> Quite over-canopied with luscious
>   woodbine,
> With sweet musk-roses, and with
>   eglantine.

And then, after long generations have failed to hear his word, and in order to show that this piece of work called man, 'the beauty of the world, the paragon of animals', is not just Hamlet's 'quintessence of dust' but has a nobler end, God says, in a new and spectacular way, 'I give you my Word: I give you myself.' And St John, bringing to the story of the birth of Jesus the deep insight of a poet, says, 'The Word was made flesh and dwelt among us, full of grace and truth.' The Word made flesh: that is to say, the whole essence of God mysteriously embodied in a human life. This Word has God in it as your words have you in them, as they contain your breath and unique feel and tell of who you are. Here is all the truth about God we need to know and it is full of wonder, the secret of the universe revealed in the alphabet of human words and actions, the words and actions of this man who revealed, both in his life and his death, the breath-taking power of God's mercy and the meaning of unlimited forgiveness.

It is that creative mercy and limitless forgiveness that Shakespeare increasingly seeks to convey in some of his plays. Use every man after his strict deserts and (in Hamlet's words) 'who should 'scape whipping?' Yet Isabella in *Measure for Measure*, kneeling to plead with Angelo, asks:

> How would you be
> If He, which is the top of judgment,
>   should
> But judge you as you are? O think on that;
> And mercy then will breathe within your
>   lips,
> Like man new made.

And six years later, in *Cymbeline*, Posthumus says to Iachimo:

> Kneel not to me:
> The power that I have on you is to spare
>   you;
> The malice towards you to forgive you.
> Live!
> And deal with others better.

'Man, proud man, drest in a little brief authority' has the power to 'make the angels weep'. But nothing, says Isabella:

> Becomes them with one half so good a grace
> As mercy does.

In one of Peter Brook's productions of *Measure for Measure* he once asked Isabella, kneeling before Angelo to plead for Claudio's life, to pause until she felt the audience could take it no longer. With the result that each night at that point there was a two-minute silence, 'a silence', writes Brook, 'in which the abstract notion of mercy became concrete for that moment to those present'. At the end of *The Tempest*, the last of those plays in which Shakespeare's theme is the creative power of mercy, Prospero forgives Alonso and Antonio who have so gravely offended him.

For Seamus Heaney the revelation came when in the poetry of Patrick Kavanagh he discovered, 'the primitive delight of *world become word*'. For us, the revelation is also the opposite. Here is nothing less than the earthing of God in his creation. Not simply world become word, but Word become flesh, *Word become world*. Here is God's Word, the essence of his nature, spelled out in terms of the drama of one who lived and suffered and died as we do; one who said that God's name is Father and his nature Love. From this moment everything must be redefined. Everything – starting with God. God revealed as Christ-like.

And by his Word man is 'new made' and the world transfigured.

Words were Shakespeare's trade. He used them more powerfully than any other writer to reveal more of the mystery of who we truly are. But he was also giving us his word: giving us a truth that lay deep at his centre and which, if he was to be true to himself, he had to incarnate in words and images and people, as God does in his Word made flesh – and giving us his word of honour: that is to say, giving us words refined in the fire of a costly life – words we can trust. Which is, of course, what God is also doing.

For in Jesus Christ he is saying: Trust me. I give you my word that you are loved. Even when life is at its darkest and most perverse. For I, too, in my Word once made flesh, know what it is to live, to suffer and to die. I am the God who is beside you and whose life is within you: beside you in your joys and your afflictions, and beside you eventually in your dying and through and beyond your death. And I give you my word that mercy and forgiveness are the most creative forces in this spinning globe, and will always have the final word.

Alone of all his contemporaries Ben Jonson perceived Shakespeare's true worth. To him, Will Shakespeare was 'not of an age, but for all time'. Never has there been a more miraculous master of his craft, with the power to reconcile what we are with what we might be; and who, by his enduring words, transfigures our world.

15

The Greatest Drama of All

ACTORS' CHURCH UNION CENTENARY, 25 APRIL 1999

Cotham Parish, Bristol

In 1959 I was an ACU chaplain to three London theatres, the Globe, the Duchess and the Fortune, and had on my hands the unlikely combination of *Beyond the Fringe*, *Hamlet* and Irene Handl in *Goodnight Mrs Puffin*. I little thought that thirty years later, in my years at Westminster, I would be conducting memorial services for Laurence Olivier and Peggy Ashcroft; or that part of my Deanery would be a room in which Shakespeare wrote.

Always known as the Jerusalem Chamber, it was built in the 1370s by Richard II. Fifty years later King Henry IV was taken ill while praying in the Abbey on the eve of going to the Holy Land, and he was rushed to the Jerusalem Chamber where they laid him before the fire. In the second part of *King Henry IV* Shakespeare (accurately) sets the scene of his death there. For six years I invited actors – Peggy Ashcroft, Alec Guinness, Judi Dench, Paul Scofield among them – to come and read their own choice of poetry in that numinous room, with all the money going to AIDS charities.

It delighted me that there was a strong link between the Abbey and the theatre, for drama and religion have always been close. The earliest Greek dramatists write tragedies about great men like Oedipus who show a self-confident contempt for a divine moral order, and their proper place within it. They demonstrate a defect that the Greeks called *hubris*, and they are punished for it. And they believed that the sight of their downfall aroused in the audience a healthy pity and terror, that purging of strong emotion known as *catharsis*. Two thousand years later, Shakespeare was to do the same with *Othello*, *Lear* and *Macbeth*. But comedy as well as tragedy had a cathartic role, and Greek writers like Euripides, by their use of comedy, showed how absurd we can often be, an absurdity recognised and purged by the catharsis of laughter. Molière and Oscar Wilde, Alan Ayckbourn and the writers of farce stand in the same tradition and serve the same purpose.

Not that drama and the church have always been easy bedfellows. At the end of the fourth century actors were excommunicated. The Normans first introduced sacred drama into England, drama closely linked to the rituals in the church, with dramatic playlets inserted into the mass at Christmas, Good Friday and Easter; but by the early Middle Ages the drama had moved into the churchyard, then into the streets of the town. There were street processions on great festivals and the trade guilds began to perform their mystery plays, each featuring the biblical stories most appropriate to their craft, or 'mystery' – the Last Supper acted by the Guild of Bakers, the Passion and Crucifixion by the Arrow-makers and the Ironmongers, the Descent into Hell – inevitably – by the Cooks. At the Reformation the mystery cycles began to die out, to be succeeded by the more respectable and much duller morality plays. Only when the London theatres were built in Elizabethan times – the Rose, the Swan and the Globe – was the scene set for the flowering of the true magicians: Christopher Marlowe, Ben Jonson and Will Shakespeare.

Now the theatre is the place where we can be renewed, taken out of ourselves, refreshed – perhaps by Noel Coward or David Hare or *Oklahoma!* – but sometimes it can do rather more. Sometimes the human condition can be explored with touching perception and with unforgettable power. In this space, if you are prepared to give your whole attention, you can be taken out of yourself and enter for a brief while someone else's world. And then you learn, in the company of others, a little more about what it means to be human and vulnerable and sinful, and sometimes tragic and sometimes absurd; what it means (in short) to be a great and wonderful mystery. 'The drama', writes Arthur Miller, 'must say with full voice what people in their daily lives can only stutter.' It must show us how life is and what it ought to be. When in 1942 an underground theatre opened in the terrible Jewish Ghetto in Warsaw one witness wrote:

Once again people laughed and cried. They cast off the depression that had been weighing on their spirits. The alienation that had hitherto existed among the Ghetto population seemed to have been thrown off ... people awoke from a long difficult dream.

Now, there are two things that most clearly define us as human beings. The first is the discovery that we are not isolated ego, spinning along from the cradle to the grave; we are persons who relate to each other because we are all bound up in the same story, this lifelong, unpredictable drama of loving and trusting, hoping and despairing, suffering and rejoicing, having and losing. Although we each play a different part, we all take part in the same basic story. The second distinctive thing about us is that we share a need to reach out to what we call the transcendent – to that which is greater and other than us, to some mystery beyond ourselves. And the way we most commonly express this reaching out is through the arts, through music and drama and art and poetry: and, of course, through worship.

So what are we doing when we go to the theatre? The director Peter Brook has written of what he calls 'Holy Theatre', or the theatre of the 'invisible-made-visible', of those rare performances that transcend our daily experience, and enable us to glimpse something which is at once both familiar and mysterious.

Familiar, for we recognise aspects of ourselves in the characters and relationships of the play: 'Yes,' we say, 'that is what it means to be human, with all our needs, all our capacity for good and evil, all our potential for revenge or for mercy, cruelty or compassion.' But we may also be made aware of that indefinable beyondness-at-the-heart-of-things that silences us and takes our breath away, so that when we go out we are not quite the same as when we went in, for we have had an encounter with some truth that causes us to glimpse things in a new light. An experience when, to echo Lear's words to the dead Cordelia, we:

> Take upon's the mystery of things,
> As if we were God's spies.

It was the novelist Joseph Conrad who wrote of how 'the artist speaks to the sense of mystery surrounding our lives – to our sense of pity, and beauty and pain'. And all great art transcends its own time and becomes our contemporary. So, for example, Shakespeare's words and characters are eternally valid because each new generation can say: 'It is valid for us; it speaks, as all great art does, of what a human being is and what a human being could be.' As does the Gospel. For the Christian drama also has this double function: it both tells a story, the greatest drama of all; and it speaks of the transcendent and reveals something of the mystery. Like all great drama, it tells a story which unites and contains all our stories in a remarkable way.

It tells the timeless story of a birth and a life and a cruel death and a rising; of a man, human as we are, who knows what it is to be at the mercy of an unpredictable world; but of one who, alone of all our race, looked into the transcendent mystery we call God and said that his name was Father and his nature was love, and that he is to be trusted, come what may.

What, then, are we doing when we come to church? We come, each with his or her own story, trying to see it in the light of this other story which has spoken – and continues to speak – to Christians in every nation on earth. This most powerful drama of all speaks to people whose lives are utterly different yet strangely the same, of what it means to trust the Christlike God and of how good may be brought out of evil; it speaks of forgiveness and of what it means to love yourself, your neighbour and your God. And this church, like every church, is a holy space, the place where past generations have met in search of that encounter between the seen and the unseen. And what we do here week by week is a kind of holy theatre. Here we are given our roles and play our part in the drama of the Eucharist. Here font and altar, crucifix and Paschal candle, tell the story of the God who shares our pain and suffering – of a world shot through with his presence, and of the new creation which exists since that first Easter Day. Here for generations people like us have gathered to enter into and keep faith with that story in our persistent, if stumbling, attempts to become what together we truly are – the people of God, the body of Christ.

16

A Ministry of Love

ORDINATION OF DEACONS SERVICE, 4 JULY 1999

Birmingham Cathedral

When in 1885 Mr Gladstone appointed the Principal of Cuddesdon, the saintly Edward King, to be Bishop of Lincoln, King's friend Henry Scott Holland wrote to him: 'Blessings, blessings, blessings! It shall be a bishopric of love.' And so it proved. So much so that it is said of a certain Master of Foxhounds that he kept on his bedside table to his dying day two photographs in silver frames: one of Edward King, and the second (only marginally larger) of his favourite foxhound.

But expectations are not always so simply defined or so happily met. When Basil Hume was summoned from his beloved Ampleforth to be Cardinal Archbishop of Westminster he wrote: 'The gap between what is expected of me and what I know myself to be is considerable and frightening. There are moments in life when you feel very small and this is one such moment. It is good to feel small, for I know that whatever I achieve will be God's achievement, not mine.' People's expectations of the clergy will perhaps always exceed our capacity to match them, and many of those expectations, of course, are invalid; yet they can weigh us down and cause us to run round our parishes, in the Psalmist's words, 'grinning like a dog' and wagging our tails ever more furiously. And that is not what ministry is about.

Ministry is about a way of seeing and a way of serving. That is to say, it is a way of giving attention to God and his creation, to yourself and to others, in order to learn to love them; and it is a lifelong commitment to that kind of service of others whose formal name is 'pastoral care' but which is more simply defined as affirming love. And those of you who are launched today as deacons will go into situations where people are deeply hungry for God yet may be almost totally unaware of the Christian story or else may reject what seems to them outdated metaphysical nonsense.

So what have you to offer? You have what you share with every other living soul: your humanity. And to be human is to be aware of what Shakespeare calls the 'mystery of things'. When the writer Philip Toynbee was dying of cancer he asked the priest on whose ministry he came to depend why he became a priest. 'He told me he had tried several things first – engineering and psychiatric nursing – but this was the first pool he had stepped into in which he couldn't feel the bottom.' 'That', he writes, 'was a wonderful answer.'

In one of Conan Doyle's stories Sherlock Holmes and Watson go on a camping trip. After a good talk and a bottle of claret they go to sleep. Some hours later Holmes wakes and nudges Watson. 'Watson, look up at the sky and tell me what you see.' 'I see millions of stars', replies Watson. 'What does that tell you?' Watson ponders for a moment. 'Astronomically,' he replies, 'it tells me that there are millions of galaxies and billions of planets. Astrologically, I observe that Saturn is in Leo. Horologically, I observe it is a quarter to three. Theologically, I am in awe at the creative power of God. Meteorologically, I suspect that tomorrow will be a lovely day. What, Holmes, does it tell you?' 'Elementary, my dear Watson,' Holmes replies. 'It tells me that someone has stolen our tent.'

Many today claim that we Christians have lost our tent: that a belief-system that has pervaded our culture, brought comfort and hope to countless millions and fashioned human lives for two millennia is no longer valid. There are however those who have chosen to go upstream against the flow of such assumptions. Not because they aren't aware of the darkness, the often cruel unpredictability of human life; not because they don't feel what John Keats called 'the burden of the mystery'; but because they believe that the Word, the creative power of God, has become flesh and dwelt – in the Greek, 'tented' – among us. Because they sense on their pulse that the true nature of God, that for which humanity waits and longs, has forever been revealed in the shape of a life, a suffering and a death like ours. A life whose only accurate description is love.

Christians confront the same world, the same problems, the same mystery, as everyone else, but we see them in a different light. We are staking our lives on the fact that God was in Christ, making our life's work to help people to see with new eyes. For in the light of Good Friday and Easter everything must be redefined: God and us, life and love and death. *God* redefined as our loving, compassionate Father. *You and I* (yes, and every pitiless oppressor and each pitiful refugee) redefined as made in God's likeness and therefore of irreplaceable worth. *Life* redefined as a journey on which we are called to learn how to trust, how to forgive and how to love; and *death* redefined as part of our journey home to God. And *love* redefined as a profound giving of attention to another person, that self-giving love manifested in Jesus. Even the *spirit of God* himself redefined as Holy Spirit, embodied as the Spirit of Christ in the new fellowship of the Church, and recognised wherever the Spirit-given virtues of faith, hope and love are found.

I want to end by telling you of the three priests, all dead now, whose example and whose friendship more than any others touched and changed my life. The first was larger than life, a natural leader, much in the public eye, his great strengths matched by equally obvious weaknesses. The second was hypersensitive and shy, an unknown parish priest given to long periods of serious depressions, one who spent time in therapy. The third was a humane and loving bishop, whose long-drawn-out death from cancer was in the end his finest sermon. They could not have been more unalike. Nor could they have been anything but Anglican. Yet each had a few essential things in common. They shared a deeply incarnational view of the world, the recognition that matter is the scaffolding of spirit, the two deeply entwined; each knew that the commonplace, when seen with the eye of the heart, is holy, and that the ordinary is far more extraordinary than we think. Each recognised the complex nature of truth, disliked anything that smacked of exclusiveness, and valued words like 'inclusive', 'speculative' and 'non-judgemental'. Each was open to thoughtful enquiry and to a wide range of opinion, aware that truth is often to be found lurking in both extremes. Aware, too, that in every church community there will be some who are so hurt or so puzzled by life that their faith is tenuous and shaky. Each was deeply human and vulnerable, for each had suffered and knew what it is like to walk in those dark shadow-lands, and people were drawn to them because they sensed they understood and spoke the same language. Each was an encourager and an affirmer. Each valued silence and daily set aside time for God. Each sought the Kingdom beyond the narrow confines of the church. And each centred his life on that taking, and giving thanks for, breaking and sharing of bread which we call the holy mysteries.

And finally, though two of them were bishops, one of whom sometimes seemed to revel in the purple trappings of his office, none of them ever forgot that at heart you always remain one who serves, and that there is one image above all the rest that all deacons, all priests and all bishops should grapple to their hearts – that of Jesus kneeling to wash his disciples' feet, and so defining unforgettably the true nature of that self-giving love which lies at the very heart of God.

Books by Michael Mayne

All available from Darton, Longman and Todd
www.dltbooks.com

The Enduring Melody

'An heroic book. Begun in health as a meditation on a lifetime's faith and experience, it ends in mortal sickness with Michael Mayne facing death. But his courage, his humour and his tone of voice do not desert him; humbling and inspiring, it is a validation both of his faith and his humanity.' Alan Bennett

'An autobiography of dying. It was brave to write it and it needs courage to read it, but the benefits are enormous. Michael Mayne belongs to the great priest-writers. He takes on the issues of mortality, both in religion and literature, and makes us all discover what pain has taught him. It is a wonderful achievement.' Ronald Blythe

ISBN: 978-0-232-52687-5; eBook 978-0-232-52818-3

God's Consoling Love
Sermons and Addresses

This new selection of previously unpublished writing by Michael Mayne has been compiled by Joel Huffstetler, the leading scholar of Mayne's work. Wherever we find ourselves on our spiritual journey, this collection of wise words will help us draw closer to the reality of the self-giving love that lies at the heart of God.

'Michael's ministry ... was a ministry of love ... love poured out abundantly, in a movement and spirit that is

faithful to the example of Jesus Christ. I am grateful to encounter him so powerfully in these sermons, and to explore with him "the secret of the universe revealed in the alphabet of human words and actions, the words and actions of (Jesus Christ), who revealed, both in his life and his death, the breath-taking power of God's mercy and the meaning of unlimited forgiveness".' The Revd Richard Coles

ISBN: 978-0-232-53017-9

Learning to Dance

Few writers have explored the borderland between faith and contemporary living more eloquently and engagingly in recent years than Michael Mayne. In *Learning to Dance* he creates a magical weave of poetry, science and spirituality, touching on the longings, doubts and hopes of all of us.

'A landmark in the exploration of contemporary spirituality ... This is the kind of book - a rare event - that one would happily take away to the mythical desert island.' Margaret Silf

ISBN: 978-0-232-52434-5

Pray, Love, Remember

Michael Mayne examines the meaning of praying, loving and remembering, and their implications for the life of the Church, basing each chapter on the theme of the collects from Ash Wednesday to Easter Day.

'A wonderfully readable mixture. Pray, Love, Remember is a Lenten book but it is not a dutiful read.' Alan Bennett

ISBN: 978-0-232-52270-9

Prayer

With great economy and elegance, Michael Mayne, one
the greatest spiritual writers of the last century, writes
practically, simply, briefly and beautifully about prayer.

Prayer is not primarily something *one does*. Prayer is
something *that is*. It is in God that we live and move
and have our being. God is always in us, waiting to be
released into expression.

ISBN: 978-0-232-53016-2

This Sunrise of Wonder
Letters for the Journey

Michael Mayne's genius was to stir the reader to sit
up and *see*, to notice the world as if for the first time.
This Sunrise of Wonder is a collection of letters written
over 20 years ago for his two grandchildren, Adam
and Anna, that beautifully and memorably expresses
Mayne's vision of life. For him, to be human is to learn
to be attentive, to recognise the mystery of people and
of things. Learn how to see, he tells us, for to see is the
beginning of wonder.

*'This is a generous, life-enhancing book, to cherish and to
keep.'* A. N. Wilson

ISBN: 978-0-232-52742-1

To Trust and to Love
Sermons and Addresses

A wonderful introduction to a collection of Michael
Mayne's previously unpublished pieces, sermons and
addresses.

With insight and wry humour he shows us how to see the things of God in art and in science, in poetry and in architecture, as well as in the scriptures and in liturgy. He makes the Christian understanding of life intelligible and attractive for people inside and far outside the churches. He teaches us to notice, to wonder, to be astonished. We learn to trust, and to love.

ISBN: 978-0-232-52798-8

A Year Lost and Found

A poignant complement to Michael Mayne's last book, *The Enduring Melody*, which was written twenty years later, in the final months of his life.

'This unashamedly is a very personal book about one year of my life and what a sudden, mysterious, knockdown kind of illness does to you and your family; about doctors and their still limited knowledge in certain areas; and about a God who stops you dead in your tracks and sets you groping for answers.'

'Michael Mayne writes the kind of theology that works for those of us who switch off when we hear yet another dry sermon or turn the pages of one more eminently forgettable book. His theology is carved, often extremely painfully, out of real life, his life, with all the experiences, encounters and exchanges which make his life – and each of our lives – unique.' From the Foreword by Sister Frances Dominica, All Saints Sisters of the Poor

ISBN: 978-0-232-52715-5